A Conversation with The Earth

A Conversation with
The Earth

Olivia Powers

A Conversation with
The Earth

Copyright © 2025 by Olivia Powers

Cover Design: Enchanted Ink Publishing
Editing: Bridgett Powers
Book Design and Typesetting: Enchanted Ink Publishing

The text type was set in Adobe Caslon Pro

ISBN: 979-8-218-65601-0 (Paperback)

I dedicate this book to

the quiet ones who have a secret garden of flowers

and dreams growing in their minds.

I exited the bland house and strolled into the lively meadow.
The butterflies welcomed me like always.
The wind grew a little too excited and almost pushed me
down.
The flowers and trees waved as I walked past them.

Once I reached the biggest tree in the meadow, I sat on the
swing it has been holding for me.
The Earth beneath the tree became intrigued with my
thoughts about our home and continued to desire my
company.
A desire for my soul's thoughts.

Today, we both will talk as the animals listen,
until the sand in the hourglass stops.

Earth

Birth is a very special, unique, and magical thing.
It brings souls into this world where they
get to go on adventures.

The woods will give each soul
a different or similar path.
And the ground will prepare
rocky trails that lead to important events.

Earth

Two cocoons get knocked down and broken.
The siblings are forced to leave the cocoon early,
way too early.
The girl's wings were not fully formed,
and her brother couldn't get the hang of flying.
The Earth had to help them the best it could,
and fast.

They were both able to fly,
after they got the right nutrients and healing.
The Earth gave wings to the girl that were unique,
but she still had other troubles with her body as she grew.
This, plus the close bond they shared,
caused the brother to stay near her when they were young.
He wasn't very good at showing his love
because he didn't know how,
but he still held her hand as they slept.

She saw how a person's soul
shows love in different ways.

Soul

My soul knows how pain feels.
My mind might not remember it,
but my soul forever will.

Earth

The soul knows more than the brain can handle.
So when the soul needs to warn you about something,
it kicks your gut and hopes you will listen.

Soul

My eyes, heart, and brain
weren't fully grown
when I was born.
But you healed me
so I could see things other can't
and spread that knowledge.

Earth

I, the Earth,
give birth to things
humans can see, touch, or hear.
I also give unclear information
that only certain people can understand.

Soul

My path in the woods started off bumpy,
but Mama and Papa Bear helped make the path easier to
walk on
by walking in front of me.
Letting me ride on their backs
until I was old enough to walk.
They stayed close behind
as I got ready to walk up the mountains.

Earth

The moon has phases that it goes through constantly.
But it always comes back full.

Soul

The soul has many houses that it enters.
The pictures on the walls show memories,
and the steps help raise you to the next level,
or bring you down
if you need to go back to a lesson.
But what happens when you get to the house
that has no more pictures or steps?

Your soul can move on once you've finished the
lessons that were assigned to you.

Soul

After falling so many times
while trying to reach new heights,
I've grown to be nervous when
I need to reach different levels.

Earth

Everyone fears something for a reason.
Being scared of certain things is important
for your human body to do.

Soul

A home is a place where people
stay and learn.
The earth is the soul's home.
You use plants and animals to show us how to live.

Earth

Lately it has been hard
to help new things grow,
because of the thorny bushes that have
overflowed the fields.
As a result of this, some have found
new methods to grow,
and I let them.

Soul

Piece by piece, we clean the ground that is filled with trash.
Piece by piece, the flower loses its petals.

Bit by bit, people throw insults at others.
Bit by bit, we change to the point where old times feel
centuries away.

Time likes to seem far away,
but it's just through the previous door.

Earth

I will never change this home completely.
The ground will always feel the same.
The trees will always be immortal.
The oceans will always provide clean water.

But it is the humans who have the ability to change it.
Half of the time, they make good changes,
however the other half destroys the home.

The ground will have too many people living in one place.
The trees' lives will be shortened as they hit the ground.
The ocean will have poison thrown into it.

Earth

How long will I have to wait
to be free from this waste
the humans made that replaced
the homes for my little friends?

Soul

You never know how deeply people care for you until you become ill.

Soul

When the floodgates open
I know not to stress and
just try my best to help the water flow.
But it is hard to be the only bird gathering branches
to give the animals that travel
through the flood.

Soul

How do we know enough is enough?

How do we know when our kindness is overlooked?

When our hard work and immense care are
not getting recognized?

Earth

The right question is:

Will your heart be able to stop showing kindness
to the people who overlook the busy beaver?

Soul

The paper plane flies into a tree
and gets damaged,
but it's the wind that helps it
fly up again.
The wrinkles in the paper will still be there.
However,
because of the wind's kindness,
the paper plane is able to continue flying.

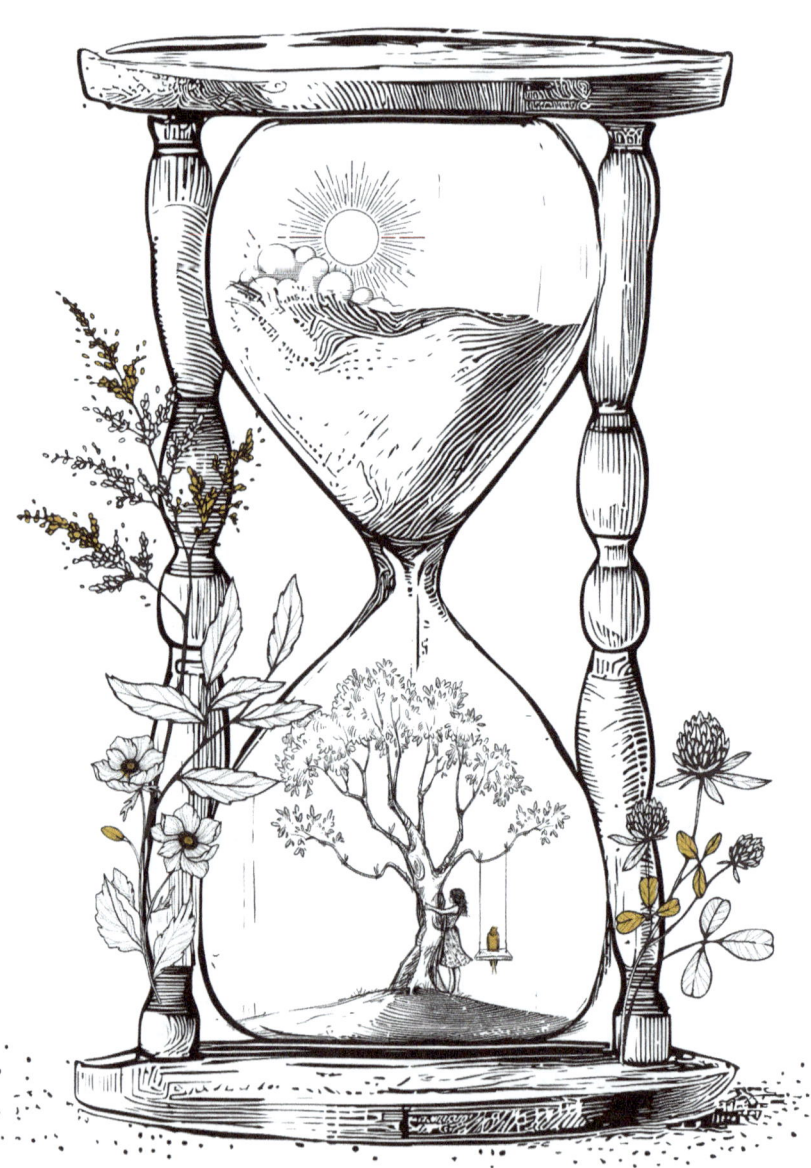

Soul

My mind is always open to thoughts.

The deep thoughts come through the door
at random times.

When I'm acknowledging them,
my mind puts the pieces of the puzzle together.

But I have no clue if these thoughts are anywhere near the
truth.

Earth

That is the most astonishing thing to me.
Your mind acts as if it is from a different time.
I hope it lets you open up to good things
that will give you more answers and growth.

Soul

If someone was able to read my mind,
I wouldn't be surprised if it were too loud for them.
They would hear the blaring noise like a party
but also see it's messy like a jungle.

Earth

People have many different
colors just like a rainbow.
People even let thoughts
cover parts of them,
similar to how clouds cover
parts of the rainbow.

Earth

As the two butterflies
that once were small
turn into adults,
they grew closer like they did when
their bodies could only crawl.
Her brother still shows his love in a different way,
and she still doesn't mind,
even if she misses the hand-holding moments.

Soul

I like to think
that he understands my personality and feelings
more than he shows.
Similar to how I understand
why he gets frustrated easily
or just wants to be left alone in his own space.

Soul

When I don't have anything to say,
I don't have to open my mouth.
When I do have something to say,
I will open my mouth.
And I will write when
I want to say something on paper,
so I can make the thoughts know I hear them.

Soul

I sit down in the silence and open my mind,
but all the thoughts are too much.
The walls get full quickly, and I'm trying to stop thinking.
Although, even when I can't write every thought on paper,
my mind continues to use a pen to write on the walls.
Making sure I remember the nervous thoughts I have.

Earth

She has the skin as light as the stars
and the mind silent like space.
She hides in the Earth,
scared of the loud chaos
of the world.
She only comes out at night,
where her silence is only interrupted
by the soft noise of crickets.

Her sister has the skin dark like the soil
and the mind loud like the wind.
She never hides.
She has the love for noise
and wishes to never leave her home,
where chaos is all around.

The two sisters rarely meet face to face.
One was born with the stars,
and the other from the soil.
When they do meet,
it is to sit with the humans who they favor.

Silence can be gentle for you,
but if her sister visits at the same time,
silence gets loud.

They favor the ones who can hear them
at the same time.

Soul

A person's soul doesn't know how to react
when something new happens.
It could react in a good way,
or in a way that affects people around you.
It takes time to get over certain things,
so give that soul the time and care it needs.
Listen to it to learn what could help it.
If you don't listen, then it could make things worse.

If the soul is not ready to speak,
give it comfort and trust.

Earth

Sometimes the fire in her dies,
but there is always a small flame still burning.
She never lets it go out completely,
so she can remember the feeling of warmth.

The fire always comes back to its
big flame eventually.

Soul

Everything breaks in a different way.

One crack in glass will never go in the same direction as another.

People's mind can break in the direction of

anger

tears

or silence.

Earth

A person's soul could
be damaged and not be seen.
That damage leaves a permanent mark,
even if it has been filled
with love.

Soul

If broken glass is fixed,
it is more fragile than it was before.

But sometimes people are as fragile
as a butterfly's wings.

Soul

The words that are written in pencil
can be erased easily.
But the words that are written in pen
cannot be erased.
They can only be covered.

Those mistakes will be in your book forever.

Soul

The world changes people.
The innocence of being a child fades away
and the Earth hides it to give it to a new child.

Earth

I absorb the things people don't need
then recycle them into something new and beautiful.
I will never absorb it completely.
The things you don't need will sometimes
poke its head around the corner to check on you
and say hello.

Soul

I have loved the moon and stars
for so long,
but I still find myself fearing the dark.

Earth

Even in the darkness, you have to keep walking.

Even if you get lost.

You will still cross paths that can help you.

Earth

But there is no need to worry.

Even when there are no clouds in the sky,

there will always be a blanket of protection over you.

It might be very thin,

but eventually it will become thicker.

Soul

The small things matter,
And yet some people just forget about them.

Soul

Don't forget to be thankful,
For thankfulness makes you thoughtful.

Soul

The small animals came around us and started talking to the
Earth.
I sat still on the swing,
face growing hot,
fingers picking at my nails.
I listened to their conversations and watched as
one by one, they went back the direction they came from.

Not taking a second to look in my direction.

Not noticing my fidgeting.

Ignoring my presence completely.

Soul

People like to ask,

"What powers would you like to have if you had a choice?"

These powers could include

invisibility, strength, or speed.

"You can only choose one," they say.

Well, I did choose one,

but I got two.

Invisibility is normal to me,

so it must be a rare power.

Although it's not as great as people think.

Earth

My little friends left,
but one baby rabbit stayed.
He looked at you, confused, as you had your back to us.
The baby rabbit jumped onto the swing next to you and
nudged your back,
getting you to pick him up.

They might ignore you
or treat you wrong,
but don't let that get in your head too deep.

Earth

She listens to everything,
and she can see things others can't,
so don't think that she is deaf or blind.

Soul

I don't talk a lot,
but when I'm excited or need to tell you something
important,
I will talk fast.
I can't seem to not do it.

Once you learn something for a long time,
it will take time to get out of the habit.
Your mind and body learns as you grow,
so if you were taught something at a young age,
you do it without thinking.

My mind learned that, if I talk fast,
I can quickly say what I want before someone else starts to
speak.
Which doesn't usually work, anyway.

Earth

It's not your fault that
you hide certain parts of yourself.
The people who made you
feel like you needed to hide,
are the ones
committing the crime.

Soul

People try to share your words and actions
with others,
but most translate them incorrectly.
Once they get translated more and more wrong,
it all becomes a lie, and you are the only one who knows the
truth.

Earth

The bird was struggling to find food
for her children before the storm came.
She ran out of time so
she quickly brought her children to safety
as the wind slowly started to grow harder.
Once the storm was over
the mother bird came out of her shelter
and found food at the trunk of the tree.

There sometimes has to be a storm so
your path can become clear.

Soul

The brain is the strongest and most unique thing in our
bodies.
But the heart has a different kind of strength and beauty.
It can get broken countless times,
yet it still stays alive.

Soul

If I ever get a chance to meet my soulmate
they will need the gift of patience as
I leave the waiting room and
learn what it feels like to have
the promise of spring in my hands.

Soul

Love gives us happiness and care,
but can also give us grief.

It's a drug that everyone tastes.

When that drug is gone,
we have to go down the path that we were avoiding.
The gate is gone,
so now we have to deal with the truth.

Earth

Your heart is a soft, fragile thing.
The desire for your heart to be held
by the rain is strong.
So make sure that you find the rain
that gently goes into your soil
and not the rain that doesn't match what your earth needs.

Earth

The rose could be hiding
thorns in its roots.
Sometimes the weed is better than
the beautiful rose.
It will be able to surround you
with love instead of thorns.

Soul

People get used to things,
but it could still hurt
just as much as the first time.

Earth

This soul isn't always nice.
She has her bad days
and bad habits.
All souls never are just that one thing
most people see.

Soul

When I can't handle the weight
of the heavy blanket that the world sends me,
the thin blanket over my emotions breaks
and water floods my mind.
In order to get rid of the water,
I have to deal with the heavy blanket first.

But most of the time, I can't get free.

Earth

Humans see flaws as an ugly thing,
but flaws are just beautiful and unique imperfections
that others might not have.

Soul

Like I've said before,
"The littlest droplet of water
helps the flower more than it seems."

But when you dump a bucket
of salty water,
the flower falls to the ground.

Make sure to understand
what the flower needs
before trying to help it keep standing.

Soul

The day and night are separated
in order to keep a boundary between light and darkness.
But lately, it has felt as if the boundary has been broken.
There seems to be more darkness than light,
causing people to get stuck in the night.
Although, plenty of people have not let the light in them be
stolen.

Earth

The economy will always have a problem,
it just takes time to fix.

Your soul has its cracks,
it takes nurturing to fix them.
Big and small.

Soul

It is fun to look out the window
and watch the leaves fall, wind blow, and sunshine break
through the clouds.
But when you have to break the window
and walk through it,
it isn't as much fun.
You will now experience the weather
instead of watching from a distance.
You have to get out of the house
that protected you
and fend for yourself.

Earth

The lightning will scare you,

and the wind will knock you down.

But always get up and

allow yourself to heal from the storm.

Taking time to heal is something that needs to be done.

Soul

What if the mountains between
the meadows and oceans
were made to protect
the flowers from the waters.

What if our souls go through
rough times to prevent unknown things from happening?

Earth

When I watch you get lost in your
unique thoughts,
I see you travel quickly past each tree
that gives you knowledge.
Some trees, you stay on longer than you do others.

You are like a bird going tree to tree,
getting whatever view it gives you
quickly before flying over to the next one.

Soul

Knowledge is forgotten and
has shrunken down to a drop of water.
Many people like to look for
knowledge that is lost
in the ocean,
but never the
dessert of forgotten tears.

Earth

The younger self never truly leaves.
Sometimes you will see it in the oldest souls,
where their younger self has been buried.

Soul

I use these conversations with the Earth
and other friends in my mind to escape.
Escapism from the world that stays confusing
and the voices that are hurtful.

But what other things could I do to distract myself
instead of talking with my imaginary friends?

Will y'all eventually get tired of me?

Earth

You can create anything with everything.
Everyone has an imagination for a reason,
so use it.

Even as you get older and don't talk to us as often as you did
when you were little,
we will never hide from you.
You made us up to help you during hard times,
so we will always use our magic to distract or entertain you.
No matter how old you are.

Earth

A old bird sits
on a fox's back and teases him
by biting his ears.

Age is not a restriction for
how you should act.
It just shows how much
knowledge you could be holding.

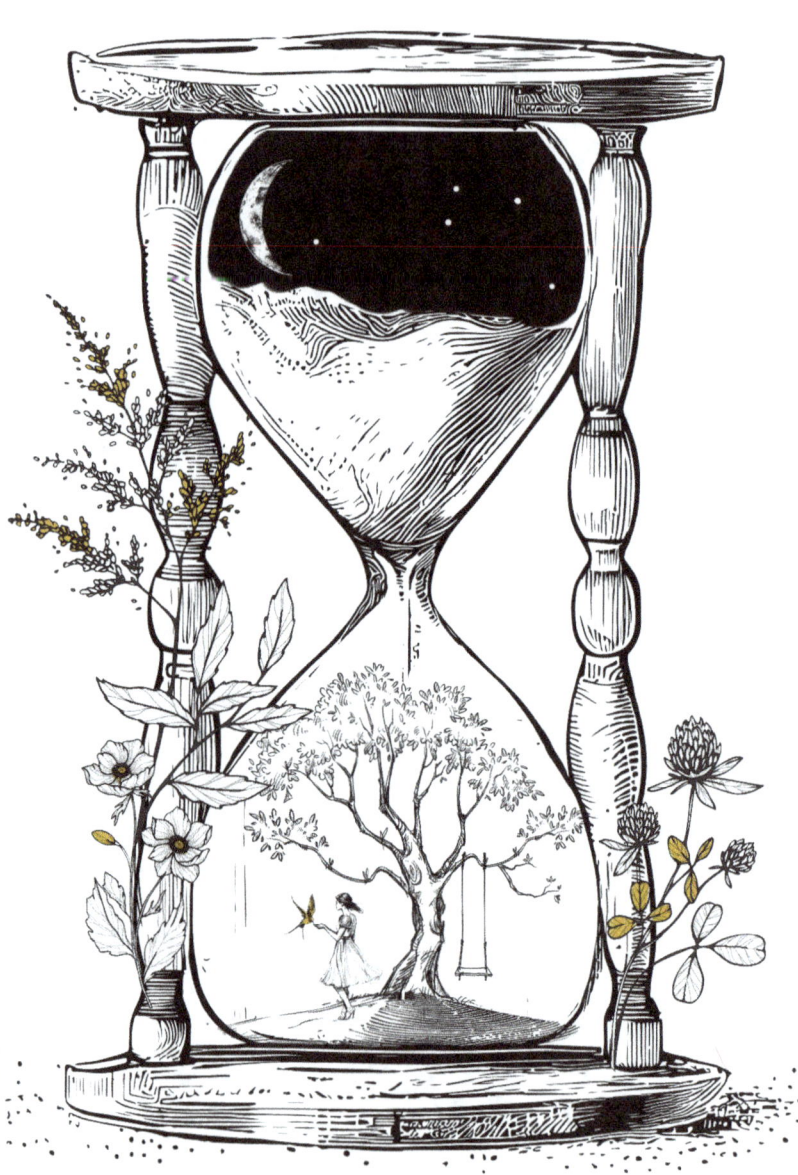

Soul

The bright yellow flowers shine with the sun
as the pink ones sway with the wind.

Waving and smiling with joy.

Earth

But trust me, child,
the inside is more tired than happy.

I'm glad I am able to make rock and soil
to cover the ground.

Earth

The grass doesn't die for no reason.

Soul

Once the tree is planted
it becomes immortal
and lives forever as its leaves
fall and grow multiple times.
It only dies when people cut it down
to gain something.

People have a habit of not only doing that to trees.

Soul

I watch as souls walk past me
with smiles on their faces,
but some minds have shadows around them.
It's not their own shadows,
it's the shadows that were made from the hurtful people
around them.

Soul

When I see someone crying,
I tend to cry with them.

My soul tends to tie itself
with people around me,
making me sensitive to their emotions.

Earth

Being enough doesn't mean
you have to do different tasks,
be someone you're not,
or do well in school.

Being enough means you are
doing your best to walk in life.

To survive.

Earth

The moon still shines bright
when it is not completely full.
It never let's go of its light
even when the darkness covers it.

Soul

Tears can be filled with soft touches
or hard punches,
just as the ocean has soft ripples
or waves that take you down.

Earth

Growth is something that will only stop
once death arrives.

Earth

The fog helps souls
pass through with ease,
giving them the keys
to the other world once they are done
with their assignments from this one.

Soul

The fog sometimes comes
when the assignments aren't done.
Some let fog bring them away,
but some have the desire to stay.

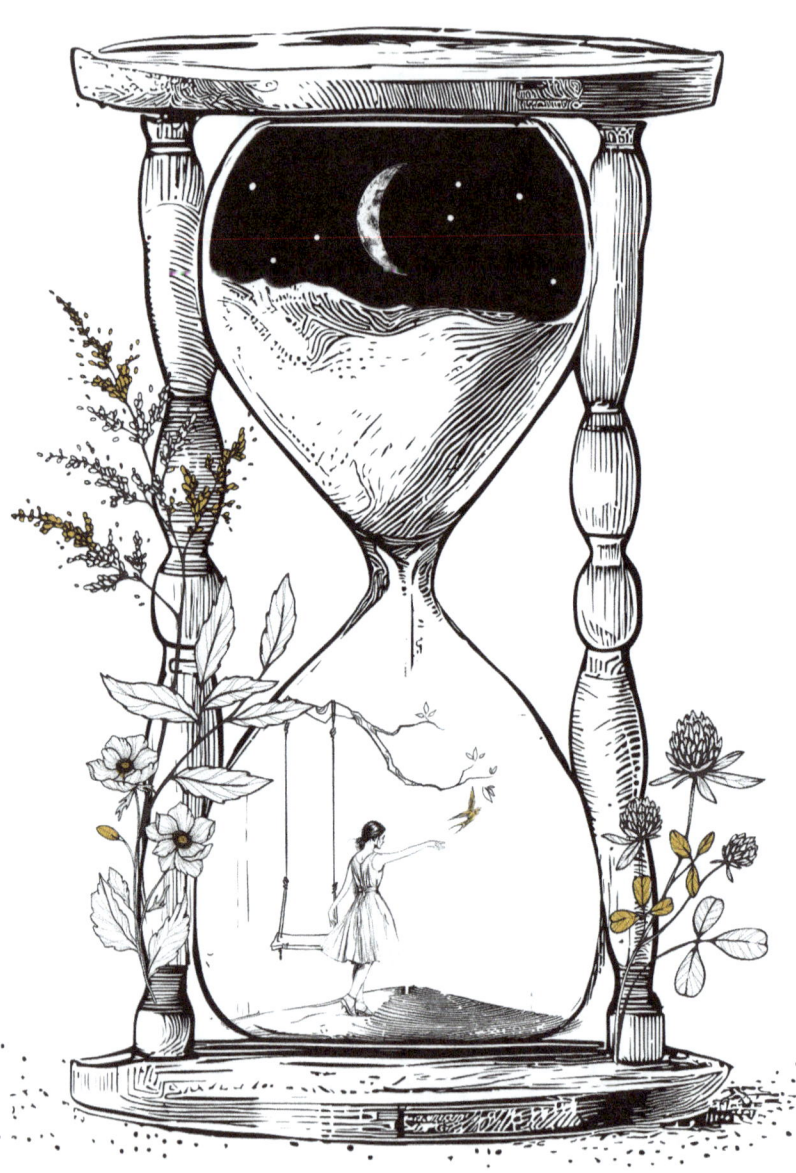

Earth

Across the river, was a family of bears.

Mama bear was in the front of the line,

while Papa bear was last.

There was

a bear who was bright like a sunflower,

a bear pretty as the moon,

a bear sleepless as a night owl,

and a bear playful like a dog.

They all watched as the bird

landed on the rocks in front of them.

Soul

Mama and Papa bear came from their homes
in the mountains and
I welcomed them with open arms.
Their warm bodies hugged me,
making my soul relax.
Hugs from the ones I love
tend to put a protective barrier around me.

Earth

Lullabies and touch
tend to calm the baby.
The new soul
comprehends these actions
easier because it is easy
for the mind to remember
the soft noise and touch.

Soul

Care of a soul is very important.
The feeling helps the soul grow healthy.
Without nurturing,
the soul will grow unhealthy and weak.

Just because someone isn't a child,
doesn't mean they don't need nurturing.
Everyone does.

Earth

I like to let the water rise back into the sky,

To get clean again,

So I can make sure my friends get healthy nutrients.

You should remember to do the same.

Soul

I sit on the swing
the only thing
that lifts me off of the ground,
but also holds me with gravity.
The vines from the earth
help hold me to the swing,
not wanting my soul to leave.

Soul

Sharing of thoughts or feelings
is hard for someone like me.
I try my best not to lose my words
in the ocean of
chaos and loud silence.

Soul

The sky becomes grey
as small drops of water hit the ground.
The leaves of the tree stay firm
not letting the gentle water touch me.

I hug my knees to my chest
as my mind dissects
the options I have.

Earth

You can keep me a secret
from the people beyond this
conversation.
Or share another piece of yourself.

The people will understand you
more than ever,
and the people who truly care for you
will be able to see the girl
behind the silence.
The world that the girl made
to do something with the thoughts she has.

Soul

The hourglass that sits up against the tree
is almost done getting rid of all the tiny rocks.

Making choices can take time if
the paths have patience in its soil.
Time is never-ending.
We just have to figure out
when the time is right to change a little detail of our lives.

Earth

She doesn't speak like she writes.

She writes it so people can hear her
when the crowd gets loud.

She found a way to speak her mind,
without speaking.

ACKNOWLEDGEMENT

I wanted to thank everyone who supported me and all of the people that helped make this book come to life. To the team at Enchanted Ink Pubishing for creating astonishing illustrations, cover design, and the formatting for the second time, just like they did for my second book "Thoughts of the Seasons." I can't explain enough how well they worked with me and made sure I understood everything. To my cousin Bridgett Powers for taking the time to make sure the poems weren't confusing and fixing any grammatical or punctuation errors. And to all of my family and friends that encouraged me to publish this book.

OTHER BOOKS BY THE AUTHOR

Life's Purest Meanings   *Thoughts of the Seasons*